REACHING FOR THE STARS

AMY GRANT
From Gospel To Pop

Written By: Bob Italia

Published by Abdo & Daughters, 6535 Cecilia Circle, Edina, Minnesota 55439.

Library bound edition distributed by Rockbottom Books,
Pentagon Tower, P.O. Box 36036, Minneapolis, Minnesota 55435.

Copyright © 1992 by Abdo Consulting Group, Inc. Pentagon Tower, P.O. Box 36036, Minneapolis, Minnesota 55435. International copyrights reserved in all countries. No part of this book may be reproduced in any form without written permission from the publisher.

Printed in the United States.

Cover photo: Retna Ltd.
Inside photos: Retna Ltd., 4, 7, 13, 25, 27 & 31
                 Globe Photos, Inc.,16, 19 & 29

Edited by: Rosemary Wallner

Italia, Robert, 1955-
    Amy Grant / written by Bob Italia ; [edited by Rosemary Wallner].
    p. cm. -- (Reaching for the stars)
    Summary: Examines the life and career of the popular singer who has successfully blended gospel and pop rock music.
ISBN: 1-56239-145-3 (lib. bdg.)
1. Grant, Amy -- Juvenile literature. 2. Singers -- United States -- Biography -- Juvenile literature. [1. Grant, Amy. 2. Singers.] I. Wallner, Rosemary, 1964-   . II. Title. III. Series.
ML3930.G7318 1992   92-16692
    [B]

International Standard Book Number:
1-56239-145-3

Library of Congress Catalog Card Number:
92-16692

TABLE OF CONTENTS

Pop Goes Amy Grant 5

Baby Amy 6

Amy Goes Gospel 8

Amy and Gary 11

Amy Crosses the Line 14

Putting Hearts in Motion 18

A Christian at Heart 20

Amy Talks about Prince and Madonna 22

Speaking to Young People 23

Amy Grant Today and Tomorrow 24

Amy Grant's Address 32

Amy Grant has successfully blended gospel and pop music.

POP GOES AMY GRANT

Lively, sultry Amy Grant is hard to figure. With her husky Southern voice, long flowing auburn hair, and cover girl looks, one would think she could give Madonna a run for her money. But Amy Grant has no intentions of becoming a sexy rock and roll star. Amy is the undisputed queen of Christian contemporary music.

Despite her association with religious music, Amy Grant has become one of the most popular female recording stars of the decade. Her albums have sold over ten million copies, and she has won five Grammy Awards.

Amy Grant is special because of the way she has successfully blended gospel and popular (pop) rock music. Though many of her songs still pack a religious message, the sound definitely sizzles contemporary. That special sound has won the hearts of many rock and roll fans around the country and the world.

BABY AMY

Amy Grant was born in Augusta, Georgia, in 1961, the youngest of four children. When she was six months old, her family moved to Nashville, Tennessee.

Amy grew up in an upper-class household. Her father was a well-known cancer specialist. Her great-grandfather founded Life and Casualty Insurance, so Amy and her family did not have any money problems. Amy even had the luxury of spending much of her childhood playing on her grandmother's farm, Burton Farm. The farm was a famous landmark near Nashville.

Though religion was a part of Amy's family life, it was never forced on her. "It was always such a thrill when Sunday afternoon grew late," recalled Amy, "and all the kids were playing outside and mom would say, 'Amy, I think we're not going to church tonight.' I loved it."

When Amy was in the third grade, she learned to play the piano. When she turned thirteen years old, Amy learned to play the guitar after she heard a girl at summer camp play John Denver songs on her guitar.

"I was mesmerized," she recalled. "It was beautiful, and I said, 'If I cut off my fingernails, will you teach me to play?' And she said yes."

Though religion is a big part of Amy's life, it was never forced on her.

AMY GOES GOSPEL

Amy was a first year student at Harpeth Hall, an all girls high school in Nashville, when she experienced a religious event that would forever affect her life.

"I was your typical young teen," she said. "I went through all the usual growing-up pains: severe acne, braces on my teeth, Coke-bottle eyeglasses, crushes....Then I was invited to a Bible study meeting. The guy who invited me was dating my older sister, and he was so cute that I thought, 'I'm gonna go to this Bible study and make this guy fall in love with me.' So I went, and an amazing thing happened to me. I encountered the Bible in a way that really affected my life.

"All these kids were really into God," she added, "talking about God as if He were a person, as if they were really *communicating* with Him. I had never come across anything that made so much sense."

Amy had already shown a natural talent for songwriting. But she wasn't thinking about becoming a gospel singer.

"What got me writing," she said, "is I had songs in my repertoire for everything by my spiritual experience, the good and the struggle it brought into my life. Then what happened is, I made a tape for my parents of all the songs I'd written, which coincidentally all had some Christian implication, struggle or vulnerability, and spiritual resolve. Nobody was putting out (pop) music about the Christian experience I was going through, so I wrote songs to fill in that gap."

Without Amy's knowledge, a friend sent the tape of Amy's pop Christian theme songs to Word Records in Dallas, Texas—the largest Christian music record company in America. Word Records liked what they heard and signed Amy to a record contract.

"I had never even heard of contemporary Christian music," said Amy. "Suddenly I felt this whole mantle of preconceived notions lowered on to my shoulders. I was definitely a normal kid who loved to go to parties, and suddenly I was traveling around the country with this huge reputation as a Christian singer. It was a heavy responsibility, because part of being young is just trying to figure out who you are."

Success came instantly to Amy Grant. She didn't struggle like most young artists trying to make a name for themselves.

"I didn't pay dues," Amy admitted, "but I sure don't feel guilty. I've worked hard. God has given me a talent, and I get out there and use it."

But though Amy was an instant success, she did have her share of troubles.

"Singing had its drawbacks," she recalled. "It often prevented me from being one of the gang. I missed that. It started at college fraternity parties where I just wanted to laugh and dance and have a good time. All of a sudden I was the 'gospel singer'... ta-dum! And every guy I knew lost any romantic interest. 'Why,' they asked, 'why is she doing this strange foreign thing?' Well, they got me wrong. I don't think I'm a prude or a stick in the mud. I've lived a very full life."

AMY AND GARY

In 1977, Amy met her husband, Gary Chapman. He was a struggling guitarist and songwriter who was trying to make his living selling his songs to Nashville record companies.

Chapman heard of Amy Grant and sent a song to her through the mail. She liked it and decided to record it. It was the first song he had ever sold.

"I was extremely happy I was going to be able to pay the rent," Chapman recalled. "And then when I met her, like all guys, I was immediately taken with her as a girl. I felt, the heck with the song—I want to get to know her."

Amy met Gary at a party for Amy's first album.

"We started dating while I was at Vanderbilt University," she said, "and we grew closer and closer through music, through God, through love. But we're not on a blissful cloud all the time. We have some slam-bang fights like any other couple."

But their budding relationship was hardly one made in heaven. Gary was having problems with drugs.

"I have been the only struggle that she has had in life," said Chapman. "I was into excessive use of pot and cocaine from the time I was around 20 until I was around 27. Amy was there for me. When I realized I was about to lose her and ruin my life, I quit."

Though she seems strong, Amy admitted that her husband's drug problem was a tough time for her.

"It was hard," she said. "Three things got me through it: support from my family and friends, praying—not so much me doing it, but everyone praying for me—and marriage counseling."

That same year, Amy released her first album, *Amy Grant*. It was an immediate hit with the Christian community, and sold over 250,000 copies. But Amy's manager, brother-in-law Don Harrell, decided not to send Amy on the traditional Christian tour.

Amy launched her career singing at small clubs.

"We never played many churches with Amy," he said. "That was the way everyone else had done it, and nobody had made it." Instead, Amy sang at small clubs.

In 1981, Amy recorded *Age to Age,* which went on to sell 1.1 million copies. Chapman wrote half the songs on that album. In 1982, Amy and Gary married. Then in 1983, Amy released her next album, *Straight Ahead.* It also sold over 1 million copies.

AMY CROSSES THE LINE

In 1985, Amy Grant released the album *Unguarded.* On the album, she used synthesizers and hard rock guitars—which was unheard of at the time for Christian performers. The album was a breakthrough for Amy. It enabled her to cross the line that separated gospel and contemporary music and reach a much bigger audience— the mainstream, popular (pop) audience.

"I wanted to make a record that musically would fit right between Madonna and Huey Lewis—joyful noise unto the Lord," she said at the time. "I realize that I'm potentially confronting a whole new audience. The Christian music realm is a family, and you can say things freely and openly with your family that you wouldn't say to a total stranger on the street."

The album reached the Number 35 spot on *Billboard* magazine's "Top Pop Albums" list. It also sold over 500,000 copies in less than a year, achieving gold status. The album went on to sell over 1 million copies, reaching platinum status.

One song, "Find a Way," was played nationwide on Top 40 radio stations.

Though *Unguarded* was a breakthrough album for Amy—not to mention a huge success—many of Amy's Christian fans criticized it. They did not like the way Amy blended rock and roll with her Christian lyrics and aimed for a popular, not strictly Christian, audience. (Amy brought on further controversy that year when she recorded a duet with Peter Cetera—formerly with the rock group Chicago—called "The Next Time I Fall.") But Amy did not see anything wrong with her music or her desire to be popular.

"There is a group of Christian artists who want to devote their lives totally to writing the music for the church," she said. "But I also feel like there's a group of us who want to be a voice in our culture. Somebody has got to be there saying, 'Hey, there are a lot of us who love Jesus, and we're going to be on the mainstream too."

"I think she wants to say that it's okay to be a Christian and have fun," said Gary Chapman. "Not completely separate yourself from humanity just because you don't believe exactly like everyone else."

Later that year, Amy Grant received a Grammy Award for the best female gospel performance. True to her controversial, offbeat ways, Amy received the award dressed in a leopard skin jacket and no shoes.

That appearance created yet another stir among her Christian fans. Someone sent Amy a box of flowers containing a note that read: "Turn back now. You can still be saved if you renounce what you've done." Though Amy had dealt with criticism often, the note brought tears to her eyes.

Amy received the Best Gospel Performance award at the 25th Annual Grammys.

"They hate my leopard jacket," she said at the time. "It sounds crazy, but the way I dress and talk is offensive to very conservative Christians. Isn't it ironic that a singer like Madonna can get away with wearing nothing but a purple lace bra onstage, and I'm in trouble with leopard spots and necklines up to my chin?"

After the storm of controversy in 1985, Amy Grant continued to write songs and perform for her fans across the country. In 1988, Amy gave birth to her son Matthew. In 1990, Amy's daughter Millie was born. Amy took some time off to be with her new family. But she wasn't about to give up her career as the leading Christian contemporary singer. Her most ambitious and controversial project ever was born just after Millie's birth.

PUTTING HEARTS IN MOTION

In March 1991, Amy Grant released *Heart in Motion.* The album was by far her biggest success. It sold over one million copies in less than a year—and is destined to sell many more. One song on the album, "Baby, Baby," became a Number One hit on the pop, contemporary, and Christian charts. Another song, "Every Heartbeat," reached the Top Ten.

But the album, which hardly mentions the words "Jesus" or "Lord," created the greatest controversy that Amy Grant had ever faced. Some Christian radio stations refused to play "Baby, Baby" because it wasn't about God or religion. (Amy wrote the song about her real baby, Millie). And in the music video, a sleek and sexy Amy Grant sings into the ear of a handsome young man who is definitely not her husband. (Originally, Amy envisioned herself singing in the video to a room full of infants. But then her fourteen-year-old nephew told her that was "a stupid idea.")

Amy had this to say to her critics:

"From a creative standpoint, it was just what I felt compelled to do. If you pick up my Christian albums, they are not straight gospel. There are a lot of love songs and relationship songs—songs that treat both parties with respect.

Amy received a lot of praise— and criticism—for her hit album Heart in Motion.

No matter what people may think, critics say *Heart in Motion* with its many love songs is definitely one of Amy Grant's best albums.

A CHRISTIAN AT HEART

Despite all the criticism she has received for her latest album, Amy Grant remains a Christian singer at heart. Before the filming of the video for "Every Heartbeat," she prayed for herself and the cast. All her band members are Christian. They meet for prayer each night before they go out on stage to perform. Sometimes Don Finto, Amy's pastor from Nashville, will fly out to meet Amy and her band and distribute communion.

"There's a standing rule that there's no drug use," said Harrell. "We have a pretty strict policy that single guys are not allowed to have girls in their rooms. We do try to uphold a certain moral code. We tell people who work for us, 'If you're representing Amy Grant, don't screw around.'"

Before anyone else accuses Amy Grant of shedding her Christian ways, consider the following facts. Amy Grant is completely against abortion. She considers aspirin "drugs" and she will not take one unless she's very ill. She doesn't smoke or drink, and she does not swear. She also believes that the husband should have the final word in a marriage.

And Amy sees the world in terms of good and evil—"what is of God and what is of the devil."

"We all would choose to live in a world built on Christian principles," she said, "because it means truth and love and kindness and compassion. Everybody wants hope. It's pretty bleak out there, pretty dark. The statistics are obvious from teen suicides and all the craziness. So what we're trying to do is take Christian principles and make them understandable. Even if it doesn't say Jesus, it doesn't matter. For someone whose heart is open—some kid sitting in his room at night, lonely, just thinking, 'My world is bleak'—that's the time that we hope our records can say something deep."

AMY TALKS ABOUT PRINCE AND MADONNA

So what does a contemporary Christian singer think of some of today's pop performers? Once, Amy attended a Prince concert. She found the racy lyrics a turnoff.

"I felt strange for three hours," she recalled. "He made a lot of references to God, which bugged me. He kept saying, 'I'm trying to be a good boy; God, I'll be a good boy.' Prince is very talented, but the whole evening was tense and sexual. It took hours to air out a smoke-filled feeling inside my heart."

As for Madonna, Amy Grant had this to say: "Madonna and I have a different emotional makeup—very different. For one thing, I wouldn't want to be seen in naked photos."

SPEAKING TO YOUNG PEOPLE

In all, Amy Grant has won five Grammy Awards and has sold over ten million albums. She aims most of her songs at young people who are struggling with life.

"So many kids write me letters," she said. " 'Nobody understands me—I'm running away,' or, 'I want to be fulfilled,' or, 'I want to be somebody.' Well, lots of people help answer my letters and make referrals, but I often reply and say that the best way to be fulfilled is to get an eternal perspective on life."

AMY GRANT TODAY AND TOMORROW

These days, Amy and her family can be found on Riverstone Farm, their 200-acre farm outside of Nashville. Amy rides horses, works in her garden, sits on the front porch with a good book, and "cooks spaghetti—the very best thing I do." Family is important to Amy. The time she spends with them is precious.

"Amy's real family oriented," said Chapman. "Her family doesn't seem to notice the success. When we're home, sitting around the table or barbecuing, she's got to get up and do the dishes just like everyone else."

"When I am a mom," she said, "the rest of the world can just fall off."

When she goes on tour—usually eight months each year—Amy brings her family with her. Even Gary joins them when he can.

When she goes on tour, Amy brings her family.

"Touring is the most intense family time I get," she said. "It's great, because in an unfamiliar environment, what else is there to do but be together?"

When she is on stage, Amy Grant is more than just a performer. Being a devoted Christian, she feels she must do more than simply entertain.

"Up onstage I feel like I try to convey my life," she said. "What people take away is up to them. Still, I wouldn't be telling the truth if I didn't say that I would hope people coming away from my concert would feel wonderfully refreshed, high on life— maybe even that their life has changed a little."

Still, Amy Grant is an amazing performer. When she goes on tour, she brings twenty tons of lighting and sound equipment. She performs with a seven-piece band and uses three backup singers.

Amy performs with an energy usually seen at a rock concert.

Unlike most Christian singers, Amy dances about the stage with an energy usually seen at a rock concert. And during her normal two-hour performance, she changes her flashy outfits at least ten times. Even her singing, often described as sultry and sexy, has raised a few eyebrows among the Christian community.

Despite all her success, Amy Grant has remained a down-to-earth woman.

"It's amazing," said Chapman. "She treats everyone like they want to be treated, which I'm not always capable of doing. And she's extremely dedicated. When I first met Amy, her aspirations were to live life, have babies, and just be happy. She didn't have any designs on becoming a big star. We're not too goal oriented. It seems like there's too much to do right now to think about the future."

Despite her success, Amy remains a down-to-earth woman.

"I'm a very normal person," Amy insisted. "I struggle with all the normal, everyday things. But I also live life with a deeply embedded sense of hope—probably because I truly believe that God is who He said He was and that He's acted in my life. My greatest desire is to tell people how my life has been touched by Jesus. But as soon as I mention Jesus in an interview, readers turn off. They go, 'What? No, no, she's getting weird. So I think I won't say it—I'll just keep singing it."

Because her Number One hit "Baby, Baby" has put her in the national spotlight, Amy Grant has received movie offers. She is interested, but has yet to commit to a project. Since she is so devoted to her family, Amy wouldn't mind retiring early.

"The other day my nephew said, 'I hope you're singing at age forty-six, just like Tina Turner,'" Amy recalled. "It took me back a little. I respect her tremendously, but in the deepest part of my heart, I think twenty years down the line I'll probably be carpooling my teenagers around. I won't give up writing songs, but somebody else will be singing them."

Amy is considering a movie career.

AMY GRANT'S ADDRESS

You can write to Amy Grant at the following address:

Amy Grant
c/o Friends of Amy
P.O. Box 50701
Nashville, TN 37204